Date Due			

MICHAEL
JOHNSON

(Photo on
front cover)

(Photo on
previous pages)

**Michael Johnson
celebrates after
winning the gold
medal in the 400
meter finals at the
Summer Olympics
in Atlanta, Georgia
in July of 1996.**

**Johnson fires from
the blocks on his
way to the gold
medal in the men's
400 meters.**

Library of Congress Cataloging-in-Publication Data
Rambeck, Richard.
Michael Johnson/ by Richard Rambeck.
p. cm.
Summary: A biography of the runner who won gold medals
in both the 200 and 400 meter events
at the 1996 Olympics in Atlanta.
ISBN 1-56766-460-1 (side-sewn library reinforced)

1. Johnson, Michael, 1967- —Juvenile literature. 2.
Runners (Sports)—United States—Biography—Juvenile
literature. [1. Johnson, Michael, 1967- . 2. Track and
field athletes. 3. Afro-Americans—Biography.] I. Title
GV1061.15.J65R36 1997   97-5466
796.42'092—dc21   CIP
[B   AC

MICHAEL
JOHNSON

BY RICHARD RAMBECK

Michael Johnson was flying. Not running. Flying. That's what it looked like to the people in Atlanta's Olympic Stadium and to the hundreds of millions watching the race on television. It felt that way to Johnson, too. "I did know I was running faster than I ever have," he said. At that point, Johnson was not quite halfway through the 1996 Olympic 200-meter final. He had finished the turn and was heading down the straightaway to the finish. He was ahead, way ahead. Michael Johnson was on his way not only to a gold medal, but to making history. As the finish line approached, he was still flying.

Just after Johnson crossed the finish line, he looked to his left — and couldn't believe what he saw. The race clock next to the track showed the winners time. Johnson had won easily, and he couldn't believe the time on the clock: 19.32 seconds. Where,

Johnson said to himself, did *that* come from? The time wasn't possible, he figured. It seemed too fast, even for one of the best sprinters in history. Johnson knew he could break his world record of 19.66 seconds, but 19.32? He hadn't broken his record; he had destroyed it! "I thought I could do 19.5," he said, "but not this, not 19.3."

Everyone watching the race expected Johnson to win. After all, he had been ranked Number 1 in the world in the 200 meters for more than four years. Derek Mills, an American who is one of the world's top 400-meter runners sometimes wonders whether Johnson is human. "I try to remember that he's just a man," Mills said. But on that night in Atlanta, Michael Johnson looked more like Superman than a man. Even Johnson was surprised how fast he had run. "I am rarely shocked by my own performance," he said, "and I am shocked."

At the end of the race, Ato Boldon, the third-place finisher, bowed to Johnson as if to say, "We're not worthy." A few months before the 1996 Olympics, the 200-meter world record was 19.72 seconds. It was a mark that had stood for 17 years. For a while, it seemed as if the record would last into the next century. Carl Lewis couldn't break it. Johnson hadn't been able to, either. But then the record finally fell when Johnson ran 19.66 at the U.S. Olympic Trials. Now it might be 170 years before someone breaks Johnson's mark.

Johnson did two things at the 1996 Olympics no one had ever done before. Not only did he set what could be the most amazing world record in track history, he also won both the 200 and the 400 meters in the same Olympics. Few runners enter both of these races. The 200 is a sprint, the

400 more of a distance race. Carl Lewis, for example, ran both the 100 and 200, but not the 400. Johnson, though, had competed in both events for years. In fact, the International Olympic Committee allowed the race schedule to be changed so Johnson could run in both events.

When the Olympics ended, Michael Johnson was the biggest star in the track universe. He had used the Atlanta Games as a springboard into history. He had done what everybody figured he would do — and more than anyone could have expected. He had also done something he was afraid he would never do — win an individual Olympic gold medal. Before the Atlanta Games, Johnson had been known more for Olympic failure than glory. At the 1992 Summer Olympics in Barcelona, Spain, he was a big favorite to win the 200 meters. He didn't come close.

Johnson throws up his arms after winning the men's 200-meters at the 5th World Track and Field Championships in Goteborg, Sweden.

Michael Johnson is a man who prepares for everything. No matter what he does, he seeks to avoid surprises. He is programmed for success. "I don't set myself up for disappointment or embarrassment," he said. He never skips a daily workout. He is always in the best shape he can be. He doesn't take risks. Ever. That's why what happened to Johnson before the 1992 Games in Barcelona was so shocking. Several weeks before the Olympics that year, he was in Spain for a meet. Before leaving to return to his home in Texas, Johnson ate dinner at a restaurant in Salamanca, Spain.

Johnson had wanted to eat at Burger King that night. Instead, he and his agent, Brad Hunt, went to the little restaurant where they had dined the previous night. A little voice inside Johnson told him it was a mistake. This time, he didn't listen. The next morning, Hunt told Johnson he had been sick to his stomach all night. Johnson, however, felt fine — at that point. On the plane ride home, Johnson learned how Hunt had felt. When he got home, he went to bed. It will pass tomorrow, Johnson told himself. It didn't. He lost eight pounds and a lot of strength.

So it was a weakened Michael Johnson who ran in Barcelona. At the time, Johnson didn't really want to admit he wasn't at his best. He hoped he had fully recovered from his illness. Once the races started, however, Johnson knew otherwise. Despite his condition, he made it to the semifinals of the 200. (He didn't enter the 400). His rivals figured he was coasting, waiting to turn it on in the finals. He never made it to finals. His time in the semifinals wasn't good enough. Johnson did win a gold medal in Barcelona. He ran a leg on the United States' 4x400 relay team which finished first.

Johnson leads the men's 400-meters race at the Mobil Track and Field Championships. Behind him are Derrick Adkins (905), Calvin Davis (151), and Ronnie Williams (800).

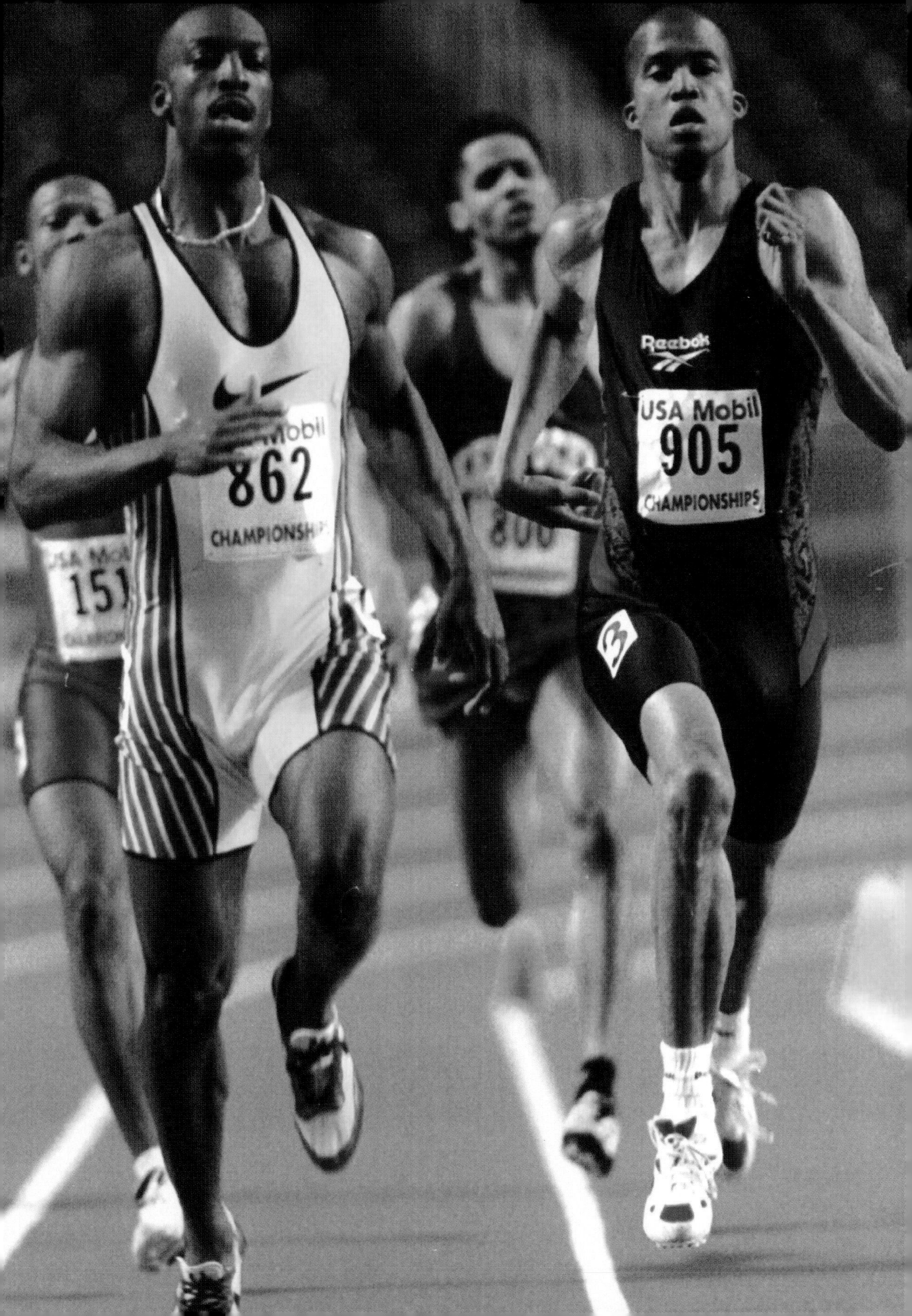
Reebok
USA Mobil
905
CHAMPIONSHIPS
862

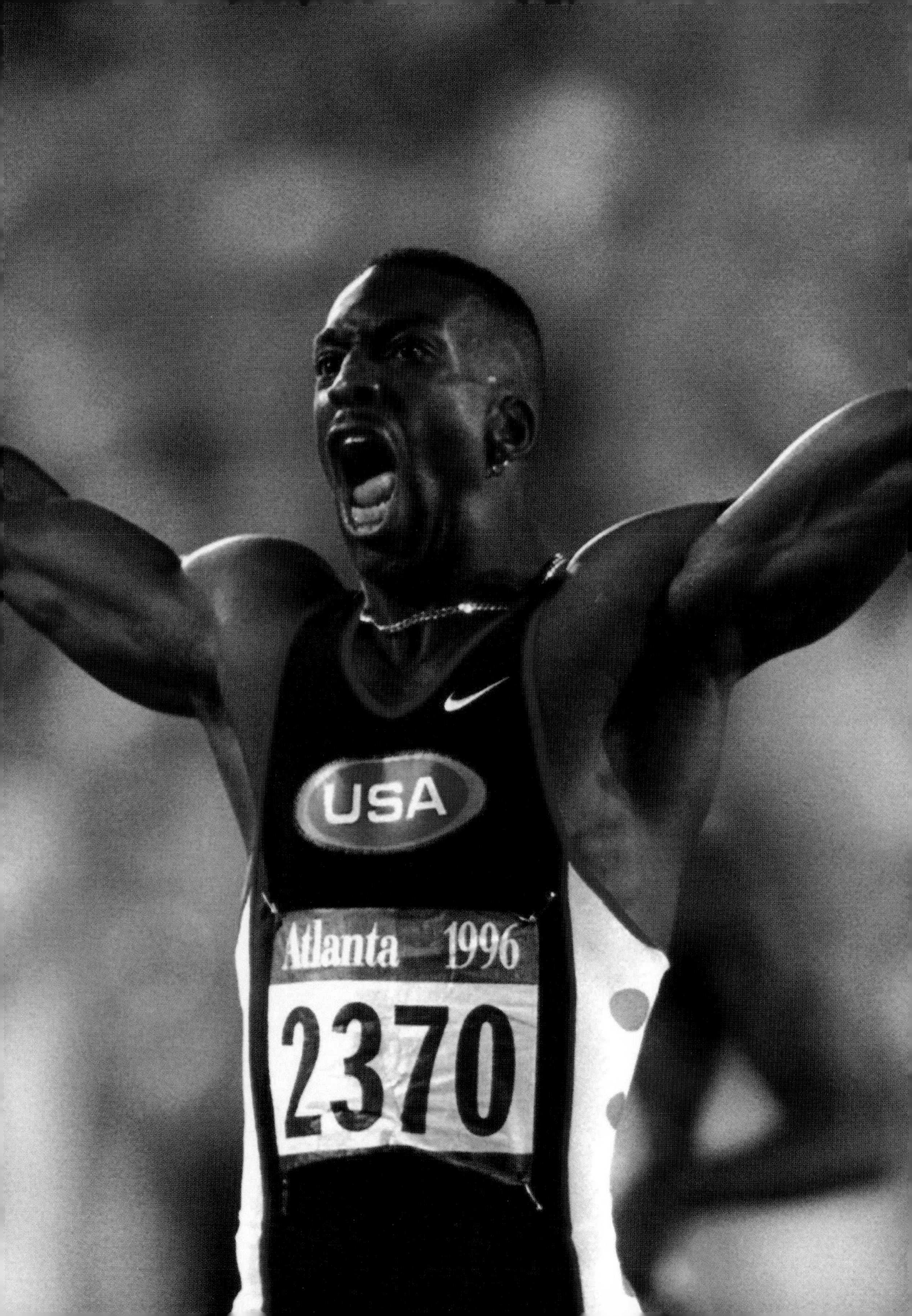
USA
Atlanta 1996
2370

Johnson left Barcelona feeling like a failure. He vowed it wouldn't happen again. He knew that when he was healthy, he was still the best in the world in two events. In 1993, he won the 400 meters at the World Track Championships. Two years later, he finished first in both the 200 and the 400 at the World Championships. Now, Johnson wanted a chance to win both at the 1996 Olympics. "He carries that burn from '92," said Tony Miller, a former teammate at Baylor University. "The only thing that'll cool him off is winning the (200–400) double in Atlanta. He started a job, and he hasn't finished it."

If Johnson wanted to finish the job, he needed help. He needed the schedule for the 200 and 400 changed so he could compete in both events without risking injury. The International Olympic Committee really didn't have a choice. Everyone knew

Johnson was the best in both events, so the IOC agreed to change the schedule. The rest was up to Johnson. He coasted to easy victories in both events in the Olympic Trials, setting a world record in the 200. But then, four weeks before the Olympics, he lost to Frankie Fredericks of Namibia in a 200-meter race. Maybe he wasn't a sure thing after all.

Johnson's start in the men's 400-meter race at Olympic Stadium in Atlanta, Georgia.

Despite the loss to Fredericks, Johnson remained confident. It was one bad race; it wouldn't happen again, he told himself. The 400 meters came first at the Olympics. In the early rounds, Johnson ran effortlessly. Once he reached the finals, there was talk that he was ready to run a world-record time. "I want to set world records in both events," he said, "but the only way to get world records is to focus on winning." He did, and he won, but not in a world-record time. He ran it in 43.49

seconds, just off the 43.29 world mark set several years before by U.S. teammate Butch Reynolds.

"The individual gold medal was more important than the world record," Johnson said after the 400-meter final. "Winning this gold medal makes up for Barcelona." Now, he set his sights on the 200. Fredericks seemed to be his top challenger. The Namibian sprinter had finished second to Canada's Donovan Bailey in the 100 meters a few days before. Bailey had to run a world-record time to edge out Fredericks. In the early part of the 200, Fredericks led, but Johnson caught him after 80 meters. The rest was history. "I have to say," Johnson said after the race, "that all that has happened here just seems impossible to top."